MAGIC PAPERS

and other poems

Also by Irving Feldman

WORKS AND DAYS
THE PRIPET MARSHES

MAGIC PAPERS
and other poems

by Irving Feldman

1817

HARPER & ROW, PUBLISHERS
New York, Evanston, and London

Acknowledgment is made to the following publications in which some of the poems in this edition have previously appeared: *Harper's Bazaar, The Virginia Quarterly Review, Midstream, The Malahat Review, New American Review #4, New American Review #7, Partisan Review, Book World, The New York Times, Salmagundi, Harper's Magazine,* and *Tri-Quarterly.* "Elegy for a Suicide" first appeared in *Poetry.*

FIRST EDITION

LIBRARY OF CONGRESS CATALOG CARD NUMBER: 70-105226

For
Catharine, John, and Lionel

CONTENTS

MAGIC PAPERS

Before we came with our radiance
and swords, our simulacra of ourselves,
our injurious destinies
and portable exiles,
                  they were here
amid incredible light that seemed
to have no source, that seemed suspended.
And so they moved majestically,
like the months, forward without
straining, not toward their goals
yet carrying them as they went,
their round limbs seeming
to exemplify what they did,
leaning out of windows, stepping from
or through doorways, bending to uncover,
lifting on their palms, carrying and
setting down, pausing to converse,
turning to where we were not yet,
saying, Here we live the victory
of the senses over the senses.

Taken, hurried into exile,
excited and flushed, chosen, delighted,
the bride beckons and inclines;
desire me! her eyes say; her hair
is combed and set in token of her reign
and servitude, her departure, her suffering.
And the day's head splits the darkness,
breaks forth, bruises her womb;
she screams; he burns and rises.
He carries a message across the sky
from darkness into darkness,
mounting furiously toward vengeance,
falling asleep so soon, and drops
the magic paper with the magic word
that falls into the chimney, into the fire
that burns the darkness, that also goes out
and no one is saved, no one the same.

I remember this: the window
rinsed clear, the droplets,
rainbabies clinging there;
the day is vexed with boredom
and correction; light shining
over here cuts like a knife;
suddenly I know I will never
again be happy in my life.
They slide, they roll down in streaks of light.
Sword in hand, the crying children,
their faces bunched like fists,
storm the highest ramparts of heaven.
What else is there to do
on miserable days like this?

I have lost the ability to sleep.
Conscience stabs my night through the sheet.
Murderer! He stabs again.
I feel for her, body draped in darkness,
defenseless, sobbing, trying
to sleep, trying to bring forth the day.
What is to be done?
I should have killed the bastard where he stood!
I make up a story without end.
The night is bleeding to death on me.
I have lost everything.
My open eyes keep open the night,
she clings to my lids.
Sleep would dishonor the dead;
I struggle to be born,
covered with blood my battering head,
my thought is misinterpreted.
I do not speak the language of this place.
I am innocent.
I scream.
If my voice itself could be
a stream intelligent of light!

I am the father of rainbabies,
shepherd of jewels, of jews,
of boys in holiday skullcaps,
shining and white.
                        With studious rapture
I lean over their gleaming shoulders
and behold the texts of light.
What pressure holds these brilliant scholars?
The swelling unison of their breaths
expounds the lesson, Light!
They say it right!
They want to run out and play;
they shimmer, they stay,
so many! they multiply,
they dazzle, translating the glory hidden
in the chill, in the thunder of voices
from the street.
                        I tap my finger
on the pane; they slide,
they run down in streaks of light.
I rage, I cannot understand my rage.
I shake the window and splash them
into darkness.
                        Am I the devil?
My seed is running toward the sea.
I laugh like hell, like hell I laugh.
I am the father who cannot reach them,
I am the sons who cannot be reached
and everlasting darkness floating between.

At twilight, mocking the season,
November in May is cold
and gleaming, excited, slithers,
lashing its darkness
over the glistening street;
the demon hangs in the tree,
laughing, eating the light,
then arches her body to show
her incredible extruded hole;
spewing, sucking back
her spew, pale belly up,
she lies with me like the Nile.
Conceive in me, she shrieks,
do not deny my womb!
From hole to hole, there is
no heart, harbor, nothing at all.
My word floats off, lost sail
dandled on the greasy wave.
So many scholars drowned!
Her gross tail pounds her turd
into a semblance of children.

My struggle to escape the idiot,
his suckers that starve my senses,
his placental calm, his resemblance to me;
he is brainless,
he is undifferentiated,
he is always there,
he is inedible,
he is faithful to the order of things,
he has no shape,
he is obsolete,
he is slippery,
he can't even say quack.
My twin, my caul.
I refuse to be two.
Use your knife, you fool! a voice says.
The one who remains will be I,
the other is another sex.
Where I cut free, the pain in my side
surpasses understanding.
I gasp for clarification.
What is reality?
The earth leaps on me.

Illness is the land for which the warriors
set out, from which return, cured, the doctors say,
of their extravagant need for reality.
The efficacy of substitutions has taught
them the existence of generalities
and boredom, that is to say, death.
They lie. The need is not extravagant,
there is no cure, I never returned.

Despair is frivolous.
                    Therefore
is there laughter in Sheol,
the hiccuping of drunken actors.
They vomit in their graves.

Only our shallowness saves us
from being crushed by the knowledge
of our shallowness.

What is the depth for which I thirst?

I make up a story without end

of the dying child who lifts
his crippled chest, his heavy thighs;
he migrates through the earth,
hunting his lost children.
They seep, they run away.
November comes, it clogs the air,
paralytic season of rain, of chaos
and asthma. Lying on his side,
he goes white in spots like a candle;
he mourns himself everywhere
and covers the earth with his traces.
Nothing holds him; discontented,
he rolls, he plunges.

Every day in each new place, he rests
in his litter, withered and golden;
messengers flash across the heavens,
blazing with the seed they bear;
infallibly, their speed hurls them past,
but from their glowing arcs they look at him.
He sees it all: their dazzling transport,
the blue sky, their tranquil diligence,
their gaze, the seed, the sun, their breathing,
the joining of heaven and earth.
There! he thinks, there should go I.
And his sole descendants, his childish tears,
splash down and waste themselves here
on this inhospitable earth of ours.

I am embarrassed. I mumble.
I blush. I am ashamed.
Before whom, stupid? Yes,
I am stupid. I look down.
I hold my hand over my mouth.
I am tongue-tied. I am too much,
I cannot.
It is comforting to be stupid,
to be confused, to look down,
to say, I do not know my name,
I am someone else's child.
I would be swept away
if I were not so burdened.
Speak to me, say
what I cannot say
that I may hear it said,
that I may say it.
I wish to unburden myself.
Kiss me. My voice
is thick, is mud,
my depth of anguish is
my depth of reservation.
I detest the wryness of my voice,
its ulteriority, its suffering
—what is not lived only
can suffer so. I wish
to give birth to the deep,
deliver myself of
this darkness, this devil.
I know the words.
I must learn to speak.

After the blood,
the violence and flowing,
after conception,
the women enter the stream,
they wash and purify,
they prepare themselves;
their distended wombs, between
two waters, divide
heaven from birth.
My voice itself
a stream of light
to bathe your bodies
and behold your eyes
Look in me! and see
what you were before
you came out of Zion
into exile
for our sakes.

THE WORD

Holding the book before his shining eyes,
he reads aloud to the prince from the sacred
texts and the profane. Clear afternoon
on an amiable terrace, beyond which: a garden
whose leisurely country gesture (its unfurling
stream, its waving boughs) accompanies
the ceremonious twittering of the cadences

of volumes that recite, within a spreading
geography of obstacles and accidents,
the fortunes of many or two or all
parted and lost, rescued, rejoined,
of persons discovered, disguises thwarted,
random journeys toward importunate destinies,
and evil that recoils upon itself
—the tales inflecting such rambling peace
as the garden discloses. All of which he reads
aloud, holding the book before his shining eyes,
while, far off, a white bird, arriving,
darts above the loftiest of the pines.

The sacred tomes, however, repeat endlessly
the one word "bread," which, with shining eyes,
he reads aloud over and over.
A bread that escapes the mouth, that dilates
in the air, transparent to the sky,
the stream, the trellised walks—so sweet,
the bread of all these, the unconsumable
one, invisible, unheard, it is
spoken bread, the unuttered silence of bread
that, reverently, he reads aloud, holding
the book, as always, close before his shining eyes.

PSALM

There is no singing without God.
Words sound in the air, mine
are flying, their wombs empty.
Whining for the living weight, they bear
themselves, a din of echoes,
and vanish: a subsiding
noise, a flatulence, a nothing
that stinks.
The glory of man shall fly away like a bird
—no birth, no pregnancy, no conception.

A people dies intestate, its benediction
lost. And the future succeeds, unfathered,
a mute, responding to no sign,
foraging its own fields at night,
hiding by day.
                    Withheld in the unuttered
blessing, God labors, and is not born.

But if I enter, vanished bones
of the broken temple, lost people,
and go in the sanctum of the scattered
house, saying words like these,
forgive—my profaneness is
insufferable to me—and bless, make fertile
my words, give them a radiant burden!
Do not deny your blessing, speak to us.

COLLOQUY

I have questioned myself aloud
at night in a voice I did not
recognize, hurried and
disobedient, hardly brighter.
What have I kept? Nothing.
Not bread or the bread-word.
What have I offered? Rebel
in the kingdom, my gift
has wanted a grace. I am crazy
with the brutality of it.
What have I said? I
have not spoken clearly,
not what must be said,
failed in using, in blessing.
I have wanted long to confess
but do not know to whom
I must speak, and cannot
spend a life on my knees.
Nonetheless, I have always
meant to save the world.

The partridge, the russet bird,
lies gently on the cutting board
between the blue bowl
and the sea-green decanter.
And a young girl is singing,
"A partridge in a pear tree,"
adding in a free contralto
all those increments that return
always to the partridge in
the pear tree. Perhaps she has
only now turned from the mirror
or put her diary aside,
roused unknowing by a second life
she has received from the russet bird.
It is like some genre painting
come alive with a touch of blood.
I note this without irony,
and I intend no danger.
One tress hanging down,
she bends over it as over
a baby she is going to powder.
I do not know for certain
that she is serenading the bird,
or why our spreading increments,
like a pear tree of the winter,
retrace, between a bowl of one color
and a decanter of another,
the crooked steps to the russet root,
while somewhere a free contralto,
perched with two lives in an auburn tress,
clothes the tree with populous song

—as I am here in a winter scene
reasoning and yet with delight,
my voice, beyond me, conjoining
with hers in the floating air;
and it is sweet to be
the bright cold sky
in winter time and any time,
and all the snow that lies between,
and the partridge and the pear tree.

1

The squared black massive head yanked
down draws the innards with it
and the slit skin, which droops
now, draggled, saddish coat tails.
The head has: obvious whiskers of eight
strange, curling barbels; three
nasty spines; two tiny
nearly sightless eyes. The lissome
delicious body lies exposed.
This she has done.

2

And now she ranges them side by side
on the wax paper: pink little gentlemen
put to bed, their pretty tails
like raven polls fresh from the bath,
neatly combed, glistening, and stiff.
Her head tilts to one side pleasantly
for so tender and unabashed a nakedness.

3

Tidy in nothing else, a primitive
aesthetic has induced her to prod
them gently here and there toward a more
perfect symmetry. All is well! And her
smiling revery is occupied with
numbering them again and again,
for all is well.

4

Dead, still their bodies arch and flip.
Heartless, headless, in what darker,

more perilous water their wandering?
A marvelous thing!
But generally quite well-behaved,
and lie still to be admired in a
wholly admirable way in their not
unattractive death. How well
they can endure being looked at!
And aptly answer her passionate gaze
by staying put.

5

Joy of the fish in his leaps,
his startled bolting, his water swilling
and low lying in the settled slime.
And other joy, of ours, in what
precipitates his narrow blood
into a less recondite, a larger
universe. Prey and morsel coincide
in death. In its relation to eating,
death is a mode of kinship, for we
are not a species that eats its food
in a tempest of wings, or wriggling,
or squealing down our throats,
yet are consanguine with all we eat.

6

Yes! the huntress returns to her lair,
dignified and wise her amble,
her mien solemn and attentive
as a courting dog's. I imagine
her quickening approach. A joyous law
hastens her stride and she is obedient.

How lovingly she carries the morsel!
It almost seems she mothers it.
The cat goes in her special trot,
a dead mouse between her jaws.
A string of tail is all that shows,
yet no kitten could be safer there.

7

And now besprinkles them liberally
—her gestures grow expansive and free—
with salt, garlic powder, and pepper,
and rolls them firmly in a coarse flour.
It is neither grueling labor nor exacting
work, and a quiet, profound pleasure.

8

A woman stands before a chopping
board, in her bloodied hands a small
cleaver. Subtly violent odor
of fish, and droplets of sweat distilled
by the heating oven, which she wipes
away with her forearm. The kitchen's
only season is summer. Somewhere
a mystery is in preparation,
but here is all the evidence.
One has done worse than fall in love
with such plainly capable hands.

SAILING CLEAR

At the reversing moment, night arrives,
summoning, engrossing the assent of all
who faithfully lie down to sleep.
And the soul strives to answer, offering
alertness, then desires and powers,
entourage of farewells dropping behind . . .

Taking the sleepers on the water,
one child, steersman and prow, guides
their island floating off amid
the wakeful waves, the solitude,
the daring flight of the distance.
World breathes . . . the banner leaps.
Brilliant with the night, everywhere
sails into place, and voices crowd, born
on the wave where light leaps clear.
Each mystery surpassed is bread
and the waking day.

Whose are the years that have come between,
your timeless future? my past without realm?
Wakeful with you, I am sailing clear.

What shall I undertake? Tonight
I am the moon looking down on you.
Look up at me from your dreaming power, child
that I was, see my mute concernful wonder,
regard me how I am: sailing, sailed clear,
I brighten the sea but with no enterprise,
without progression because without faith,
vowed, but to no task commanded.

Sleep, my world! we are setting off
in the streaming night. Nothing can be lost
of all this drifting power, from which no creature
turns aside in this our recurrent time
that is declared anew the night and the day.

POET AT THIRTEEN

I

Sun and water. Sun on the water, darkening.
The blue and the gold.
By chance, they were his school colors.

Item: The Catholic Church is not a sexual institution.
Item: Black is the color of mourning, not love.
Item: Come, lovely incongruous death!
Item: We are all liars.
Item: We went and tried to peek into McLaughlin's Baths.
Item: The fair desire the brave.
Item: All colors are the color of love.

And westward from Jersey and Richmond, the sun
transmits from heaven toward his vital shore.
Blaze of allusions at their strenuous play;
its arrows, far-fetching, indicate *him*.
"Sailor boy, marry me!" the rippling sirens sing.

The basements gape, disgorge
pig, shock wave of stale and lard,
the fart of darkness.
Within, corsetless,
an old Negress mumbles in slippers,
carrying a dish and spoon; peers out.
Crazy hair. Dirt eyes like neglected moons
just level with the street.

Twilight thrills; the sweetheart ascends, her dress
dainty, dirty perhaps, dim-pink; avenue
glaucous and tempting; seeing herself seen,

her wide lips are pressed back, not looking
around, making a face; shame-shambles.
Moon odors.
Venus at twelve, browner than sweets.
A milk bottle tightens her hand, swings it.
Every little errand brings its Rachel to a well.

Trembling with a seven-years servitude,
he seals an envelope, sacrificing to Mr.
Walter White two personal lovelorn bucks.

2

See him that night at the red-
glass lamp, round comfortable mother
of his dream life, culture, like dandruff,
flaked on his brow, cramming
a sandwich, devouring Turgenev and
Tolstoy's parables. Where love is, there
he is also, skimming the steppes, seeking
flesh of his flesh before the snow.
A heroine paces the Russian gardens,
the wind heaves restlessly, retreating summer
snivels along the ground; moon of 40 watts.
Deserted, she craves a devastating freedom.
Even her hair is pale. He vows love
undying, of her skirts noting that
they're more real than her legs: decidedly,
she is not a *little* girl! And inasmuch
as ye have done it unto one
of the least of these my brethren . . .
Savaging her salvation

from cars, from drowning, from public scorn
and racial rebuff, from a banging
by the crap-faced bookies fingering their change
like nooky and belching the candy store . . .
Sonsofbitches! He gets them the hell out of there,
to productive labor in a muddy village
of the hinterland. Rushes back, just
in the nick! Desiring danger! The book
slides down.
               "What *you* lookin' at?"
She trucks on down the arbor, hovers
at the end of the long alley, reclines
compassionately.
Their tender gratitudes, commingling within
the glowing limits of a lamp, resurrect the rolling wave:
her whitest, most scalloped, most carefully hemmed slip.

    3
Agenda for Further Studies

Item: The sweetness of life.
Item: Must this be confused with fatuousness and conceit?
Item: Know thyself.
Item: An art of happiness.

FOUR PASSAGES

I. BRIGHTON BEACH LOCAL, 1945

Hot Saturday expands toward twilight,
Spacious and warm. Their train, at the end of the line,
Haltingly departs from Coney Island,
And settles, after an initial whine,

To a lulling commotion, with which they, too, move,
He sixteen, she almost a year older;
They have been swimming and are in love,
And sit touching and rocking together.

Exercised and sober, their bodies are
Rested, tingling, refreshed and grave, compel
The tautened skin; he is freckled,
Her complexion of the Crimea

Is healthy olive-and-rose, her frequent smiles
Transcend what is perhaps a pout or the faint
Ruminative suckling of a child;
A severe and orphan dress disdains

The completed opulence of her body. Stretching,
They vie in banter with sunburned strangers nearby,
Break off, having acquitted themselves
With honor. Pride completes their pleasure.

They are indeed proud: of being lovers,
Of their advanced and noble sympathies,
Their happiness, their languorous wit
That rivals dignity, ripens pleasure,

And candles failure in the subway faces,
Restores their opacity with kindly justice;
Imagining their competence exceeds
Every foreseeable occasion.

These are young gods defining love, banqueting
On glances and whispered smiles and amiable
Raillery, and believe inexhaustible
Their margin for error, and summon back

The solicitous waiter, command another course
Of immortal tenderness and levity,
Drunk and dazzled with love, twining fingers
On a summer evening after the War.

Fixed in force, the train persists on the ways,
Its windows intersect the streaming darkness;
Their expanding revery engages
Almost the first apparent stars.

A cunning and subterranean will
Even now detaches them toward other destinies,
Misery, impatience, division that shall
Complete their present and mutual ignorance.

2. MEETING HALL OF THE *Sociedad Anarquista*, 1952

The rough wooden floor impedes the dancers,
Who, unable to glide, move by steps,
And, warmed by Gallo wine, gain speed, their pleasure
Neither false nor excessive, though uncertain.
Too sparse for the loft, the rest, making many,
Crowd the phonograph and wine jug on the table.

Folded chairs are ranked along a wall;
Atop the shelves, the dying pamphlets,
Absolute with ardor and fraternity,
Receive New York's gray intermittent soil,
Dust: A few Spaniards with weakened eyes
Desiccate in the fadeout of history.

Tonight, under the toneless light
Of usual guises, young friends have gathered
With festive desire to welcome a friend,
A woman fiery-looking, childless, and stubborn.
Embarrassed by gloom, she sits on the floor
And smiles her description of famine in Italy.

These two who dance have met since parting, yet,
Because she has come alone, because he, too, is,
Like one recently divorced, freshly marketable,
Novel with the glamor of commodity,
A vividness revises his elder desire,
Selects her cropped hair with loving recurrence.

Her response is rare volubility,
Her conversation challenging, obscene,
Embittered or descends to jokes or glorifies
Giving, pictures Nietzsche dying for want of love.
It is quite certain she does not like him, certain
She wishes to please. Her caricature boringly enacts

A passion genuine and chaotic. Wearing red,
At twenty-four having desired, having failed
To be reborn a Negro, Israeli, gypsy;
Devastated by freedom, her uncompleted soul
Retains its contact with psychosis and with
The incredible softness of a woman.

Her manic vehemence drops. Dances off, gazes,
And says he looks sad, and to restore his spirits
Offers the nursery of this body she
Exhibits and detests; her pity and her guilt,
Like children deprivation has misled,
Hold hands tenderly, without affection.

Before night ends, forgotten at two by a mad
Mother, dragged along by her father, lodged
With orphans, she jumps, denuded, gleaming,
Nervous, from the bed, and producing
Her repertoire of wifeliness,
Asks would he like a book to read.

3. AT PASHA'S FIRST AVENUE CAFÉ, 1954

Three walls are tin enameled; on the fourth,
a spreading country all sienna and curves
offers in conventionally edible style,
and half-eaten already, glory that is Greece:
a bit of marzipan sitting on a hill
—it is the Parthenon; beside it, Delphi's vale
whose lovely oracle from her picnic table,
foretelling free food, expensive manners,
teaches the very gods not to grab,
while lots of girls, consuming the sun's output
of yellow, dance madly over the flowers, or caress
those half-human heads upon their human laps;
symmetrical and white, a splendid mountain
overlooks it all, though shaken, it might seem,
by inspired tremors from the artist's hand
which fluttered like a bacchant who commends
Pasha's friendly pilaf and beautiful wine.

Dull, but fathers, and exotic in a faintly
swarthy way, and practical about their women
who can't let anything alone with their long noses
and short fuses, their dish-busting politics,
and their big mouths and spitefulness and vanities
—vaguely indifferent, they take in the dancer's lousy
American style, from whose disorder they infer,
by casual and well-known processes, the exact degree

of her voluptuary value: how hot in bed,
and with careful Mediterranean lucidity
thank their gods she's no Greek's daughter
earning so little for showing her stuff. Roused,
at last, from their revery, the sensuous shade,
they shout advice, encouragement, praise, keeping
one eye cocked at what figure they might cut
and wondering if she's maybe not there in the head.

Intolerant of the abstract ritual,
Her dancing too portentous to entertain,
Inept, overt, offensively familiar,
Breathless in the burdened unreality,

She fights toward the pure, the undemanding
Air, toward flight, aching to inspire endless
Rebirth, a plenum taut with plentitude,
Of her virgin children the virgin child; messenger

Struck dumb, nailed to the stage, staggers
Through attitudes that crazily conflate
Sexual homiletics with moral coquetry;
Her gestures heave, labor to translate

The unreality: tempt, placate, challenge,
Exclude toward a universe of love and giving . . .
Unaware that her sacrifice proceeds
Beyond her power to surrender. The audience

Stirs, its attention irregular, vague,
Its judgment unfavorable, its indifference,
Like the gods', capricious but final.
The tiny uterine increments transcend

Her body: a stillness flickers, neither
Reposeful nor dancing, the emptiness
Affirms itself in repeated nothings
At one with the judgment upon her.

4. PARTY ON EAST TENTH STREET, 1955

Their party has romance for its occasion,
A courtship of roses, Saturday's roses
Hilarious now in the violet air
And whom the dance encounters with loves
In a folly of poses gravely swimming, alluding to,

Deferring, always to them, though importunate
Sometimes, begging their arms, their tresses,
      their kisses. Kisses
Of the rose, how little they endure! consumed
In movement, their plays revived as the air's
Repeated caresses that pursue with music

The weakening, dizzied roses faster, farther
Through misleading groves of alarms and despairs.
How cold there, frightful and lonely! till they cry aloud
And are consoled, while the music slows, by a voice
Lost and found in the voices of their holloing loves.

The roses brighten and withdraw;
look down, smooth, correct,
amplify their persons,
these speaking modesties
of linen or of silk

wherein are nursed and hidden
the infant revelations
whispered to their beating hearts.
Given and giving this
only, untouchable elsewhere
but touched by a mothering voice,
because of whom
the roses love and are lovable,
having consoled their despairs and tears,
their fragile lament, and made coherent
the gaze of discoursing intelligence
that dallies brightly now among the roses
and their loves, and in the party's
boisterous charade invokes
a mother invisible beyond
the blood that gathers at the root,
the light that wakes the flower's
flower.

What strange animals we are!
                              Responding
to slaps and losses, teasing, kisses; eager
for contest, for smiles of shared intelligence;
witless, disheartened, drooping in solitude,
desiring sights, and the seeing of other eyes;
nourished by news and touches, crowding
the air with spirits and revenant loves;
asking of things what beings they possess;
compounding the soul of others or dividing
in a drama of voices, preferring guilt
to terror, terror to isolation.

34

Of hunger and thirst a king dies amid
fountains and gardens.
                        An infant, isolated
within the circling intelligence of love,
has died.
                    What strange animals we are!
                                    Smiling
with the roses, held in their garden glances, he
receives intelligence of her, husbandless,
motherless mother. One now and now together,
they mime her gestures—goes
wandering, the infant across her arms
offered in the empty street.
Does not know how to feed it. They squeak
its little cries. Their eyes glaze. It sickens
and dies, curling like a leaf
amid their banquet of smiles.
They hide-and-seek,
cannot let her go. They clothe
themselves in her chill. Starlight
has estranged their faces.
Recurs, surviving in a stupor
beyond heartbreak, gnawing
her blue, delicate, negative
lip; she does not cry
or turn away: radiant with
no seeable light, breathless revenant
absenting in a poverty of desolation.
                                From such
it shall be taken to the very conclusion
of time without mercy or remission.

                                    This one
is interesting: scrubbed pink yet oddly drab,
her articulation foreign slightly and
indistinct, direct, awkward in the dance,
stocky, broad-basined, touched with a violet glow,
and wanting, he knows, to be taken home.

Around each rose a specter glows
Bluish and biting, after the fine
Electric wit departs from it.
Odor of ozone concludes the feast
And leaves the rose its cold repose.
Spreading in darkness, the specter is the rose.

AN EPILOGUE

She has been met by others since.
They say she gardens for a living,
her manner hearty and masculine,
was married for a time, sleeps
around, though less now than before,
is given still to brooding and rages,
but faces middle age with greater
equanimity than she lived her youth,
has altered her name and has good
color, dresses better, preserves
an interest in the theater, is less
vulgar, somewhat commonplace,
and more optimistic than not.

DUNKERQUE 1951

Lazy or careless, he drops
out of this life to those lives
—too dry to nourish, thin for shelter—
his own and others',
where the animal cry, leaning forward
—quick, dangerous, nonplussed—lingers

at low tide, and over the noonday beach
they come running, in the distance flowers
but whores when they arrive
at shipside in wet bathing suits,
hugging their purses and clothes.
Blondie, Red, and crazy Lulu
foulmouthed, swindling, ready to fight.
Breathless over cigarettes, among
the sailors gone green between desire
and spite, hungover underfed,
lowest of the low,
they fly at the men, clawing
their rancid face with the gull's
covetous voice, unremitting, voracious.

The soul set spinning to starve and freeze,
stranger nothing fits and nothing feeds.
Or is it—stupidly—
insensitive and fastidious?

THE FATHER

No voice declares from heaven. Must
we, too, acquiesce in the appalling
ordinariness of this man,
his heart failing and nothing to say?
Awaking, snappish, resentful, confused;
sitting with knife and fork at noon
in judgment on himself;
aching toward dinner, poor boy, newsboy,
fatherless boy, cut clean through,
dying for affection—yet proudly declining
to present his bill to his Maker
(however prudently refusing
to tear it up). One almost smiles
to read of it, although one has,
to tell the truth, sometimes
been a shit, however inexplicitly
complicit, *n'est-ce pas?*

Dying in earnest—as he was earnestly
doing—we are led to ask about
the Maker of the lion and bear,
the infinite night-shining star,
O bright and brighter than before!
and creatures who go here and there
entangling well their various ways
on this our simple shining star.
Who is he? and by what right made us
not as we are not but as we are?
or lost us so that we are neither?
And must we leave these ways, this shining,
such creatures, and the lion and bear
to his bad accounting and his inconstant care?

39

Humiliated, his ambitions broken,
and never, certainly, a lion at heart,
he sweetens what little he can,
tramping the low domestic earth,
hero of the hearth, the garden's guardian,
carrying the groceries in,
setting them down, brewing his own, pleased
in the pleasure of daughter and son, turning
the TV on, turning it off,
turning it back on,
punctual and solvent and undecided,
meaning none of it,
or standing dazed among the peaceful summer
greens, almost in the distance seeming
an ad's beatitude: idiot-consumer,
aging, awestruck, meek, and grateful
for the profuse and profound rightness
of all this wrongness.
                              Beyond pain,
pessimism; beyond
that, his heart cuts back
—the vise's blank ferocious fix:
fear, bewilderment, betrayal,
enmity, despotism, whatever
he swallowed or spat, all of it,
he bends and crushes together
in a powerful shrug savagely suppressed.

I will tell you a story, it goes like this.
With waistcoat and a watch (the enormous one
that ticks so heavy, wound down

as ever and running slow), he hurries
into darkness (oh, too late! too late!)
toward a party by now long over,
the garden cleared of cakes and tables,
the little celebrants packed off to sleep
or sent out sleepily to wander
in gloomy lanes, or under hills
that slope away among stones,
led forward, poor dears! by a fictive light.
Tender and round, busy, abstracted,
everything on his mind and his mind
on nothing, quickly pleased, easily affrighted,
he hastens after, unable now
to catch that small courageous band,
hurrying badly and reeling forward,
tired, it is true, yet not disheartened
on his forsaken way where no star shines
and their laughing chatter long since faded,
faded then and reappeared, roaring in lanes
and on the hills, then reappeared and faded.

The pain of it does not ease; this is
too much, we say, let him have known
before the end his glittering scene:
himself poised with shotgun, two yelping
beagles in a snowy field, a rabbit
never too soon forthcoming from brake
or burrow, the sky total and unexpended.

THE HEIR

He is a surgeon resectioning the heart.
Confessedly dead, yet the corpse
sits up and shouts at him, "You idiot,
do you know how to do anything right?"
And tries to grab the knife or the dream itself.
It seems to him they are struggling over
the very nature of reality.

On the bed awaking, he who was the doctor
is now the patient. So short the life, so long
the convalescence! Sad, square, and aching,
he accepts his father's dead heart, commonplace,
appalling, and the old man's misery and maiming
return in the son's chest to their brutal beating.
Devoted and good, his normality resurrects
in dull parody that bitterness and failure.

Unloaded, held to the head,
the catastrophic life clicks repeatedly
in the empty chambers.

                        Sitting in our room now
and carried away for a moment, he says, as if
repeating an important lesson, earnestly,
with yearning and with pride, "Actually,
Dad and I have the same sense of humor."

REREDOS SHOWING THE ASSUMPTION
INTO HEAVEN OF FRANK O'HARA

Farewell, sweet Pinocchio,
Human, all-too-human child,
Dead on Fire Island
Where the bad boys go
On making asses of themselves.
Death ought never have made you good
By altering your flesh to wood.

Thrust from our theater of cruelty
By a happening of fate,
The mad butch-taxi
That drove you into a state
Alien though near, too like us though far:
O supernumerary and star,
In the bright with-it summer air,
Your impromptu on surreality
Is worthy of our universal flair.
Garbed in death's sticky drag,
Out flat like a *déjeuner sur l'herbe,*
Your body's nakedness will not be late
For its brazenly touching date
With a corner of the Hamptons' turf,

While talents of the *Tout-New-York,*
Catered by a mournful museum,
Entertain eternity before
Your blue eyes' novel tedium,
And ascend from breadlines to headlines
To mumble to your catafalque
Heartfelt idiocies.

Toward cosmic in-jokes like this,
Your attitude is perfectly correct:
Flat on your back looking flat up.
You would have disapproved
Our solemn squish, but

Your spirit now, caught
In a sharp, ascending draft
And crowned with the lyric hair
Of Saint Apollinaire,
Sweeps off to Dada-glory
Amid *sons et lumières,*
Musée of Infinite Inventory
Where all pigments are a sweet
Supplice-délice,
And the lovely paintings leaning
Gaze down at our inferior world.
Lounging in open corridors,
The statues loiter to discourse
In alexandrines that beguile
The covert Muses in the peristyle.
You will write, at last, in French,
And with endless lovely women,
Fleeing their heavy husbands' exigence,
Play duets upon the piano.
Your Curatorship will be
The *Catalogue raisonné des derniers cris.*
Assemble, collate, file, remit to us,
Via pneumatiques of heaven-sent confetti,
Your final views of our sad Cosmopolis.

SEEING RED

Twice a week, fantastic and compelled,
beyond the half-drawn window shade, voice
ablaze, she yanked a suitcase off the bed,
unloosed the death ray of a drop-dead stare,
the parting gusts of her furious red head.
"You'll see!" she screamed and slammed the door.
So?
      So nothing. She crept back in
and cried and fell asleep and slept.
A lion was on the landing,
a mouse was in the marrow inching.
Cornered, she poked at the burning eyes,
she spat at them, she hissed.
Fury and Misery.
The lion leaped and tore her thighs,
mice were gnawing in her feet.
A restless girl, a rotten period.

"Feh! She talks like a mocky."
                So, my sisters
while we lie and peep across the airshaft.
Then I, like the summer dawn's ambitious sun
—eager to shine and burning to please—pink
with preference, ignite my gift for scorn
in the vacancy of understanding.
(Let them be praised! these red-haired sisters
who taught my senses' prosperous bride
the famine arts of transcendence:
bitching, snobbery, and condescension.
Their smell, the pale juvenile nighties,

45

the bloodlettings of their reddened fingernails
on passionate mornings—damp and idleness
and tempers and kicking in the tangled sheet
—brought me to a woman's country
of warmth, disorder, and cruelty,
biting envies and a smoldering shame,
so that I don't know yet if my mockery
is defending a privilege or a pain.)
My act is idiot approval that stings
her sleep. *I* am the little devil spurred
to spank those cheeks and rout her from bed,
nerves afire with sarcasm and applause.

2

One day, I think, driven as always,
she got to the door and didn't stop,
set off with her squat delirious suitcase
to wow America, or marry
—like an absentminded salesman,
his dirty wash in the sample case,
and they want it! they buy!
Who needs talent, with such despair?
What else is America for!
Bad news, bad breath, bad manners,
the grievous suitcase marches on,
prophesying from every corner.
"Betrayal!" it screams
and snaps itself shut.
What a start in life!
those scraps of rumpled underwear and clothes,

sloppy habits, bad teeth, a roaring tongue,
a crummy job and worse marriage.

3

Straddling your freckled shoulders,
riding high and sly in 'sixty-nine,
smiling (no less!) and sentimental,
each time I shift gears, underfoot
I feel your wronged hysteria
revving in the block. What
have they done to your gut?
                              Cracked
moon, homeless gingercat,
I want to take off on you,
pilgrims to nowhere,
streaking toward skid row
and failure like the vast frontier.
My young heels drum
excitedly on your tits.
At midnight you awake and cry,
My pride is injured,
my soul is empty,
my heart is broken,
my womb has died.
O my brother,
avenge me!

Rising beyond the pane,
red and pale, feverish, gaunt,
burnt crust but raw dough,

you grip your satchel
and leap through the window into
the middle of the Great Depression,
your eyes endowed with total misunderstanding.

4
Would it be too fatuous of me
and too late, too squeamish, too phony,
too perfectly American,
touching three small fingers to my brim,
to say across thirty feet of foul airshaft,
thirty years of life, "Help you with your bags, Red?"

THE WARRIORS AND THE IDIOTS

Our themes were three: defying dangers,
triumph over dangers, respite
from danger. And weapons, four: knife
and light, blood and the burning maxims:
Stain a breast before you foul your pants.
Pay twice the price, if you pay at all.
Defend father and mother, kith and kind.
These others were not warriors: ninnies
and nuts, the palsied pencil vendor,
mongolians, morons, the dwarf. Strewn about
like pumpkins, squash, or stumps grown over
with moss, they lay quietly beyond
the law, observed no imperative,
enacted no command, these children
too cruelly punished in the womb
to endure a second forfeit. Stultified
by the darkness of the forty days, they had,
as if tumbled from a broken crate
or shivered constellation, rolled to a stop
in the sun, like damp oranges, like fallen moons.
Wherever we went, their grunts admonished us:
There is no victory, there is survival.
No, there is only recollection.
You think you have survived because you can
remember when simultaneously
you were swimming and drowning.

Even the Messiah of dogs and cats
will overlook them on his final errands
through the streets, and Paradise take place
without their spoiled hosannah, they content
to remain at any angle whatsoever
in the sun for all eternity.

NIGHT AND THE MAIDEN

The children run away, they hide,
teasing the twilight on the leaves,
they scatter under shadows, their eyes
blink out, their voices vanish.
She follows and calls them in to sleep,
her cry impatient, but hears itself,
is astonished, flirts alone, succumbs,
desires labor and a second solitude,
and rises to compel the listening stars.

Toward her the stars send forth their night
—prince, husband, stranger, death—
bearer of the dark illustrious names.
He overtakes her in the wood.
She is startled by the dark pursuit,
a brilliance fallen too close.
Having come so far tonight,
leaping over all the ways,
dropping toward sleep, he draws
his darkness from the sky to light
within the empty heavens of her flesh
the lost inviolable stars.

ELEGY FOR A SUICIDE

1

Behold, these flowers of the field,
how deft they are at their windy games!
Unjustifiable, unjustified,
they are not weeping,
while you stand apart, growing thin
among the prattle of the flowers, their tidy,
childish sentences:
                         Naughty! cries the daisy.
Yes, you pumpkin! the other replies.
Will you give me one? asks the rose,
for me and Linda?
And bend together gossiping, telling
the sweet things they have eaten.

2

Feeding the children, we overcome chaos,
their eating blesses the food, blesses
the monotonous manna of our lives, feeds
our hunger for meanings. It is our commonest
form of prayer, naming the bread-word in the bread.
The blessing, too, they eat; the blessing's blessed;
eternity emerges at its growing point.

3

Tyrants, these girls convict their lives;
ruthless, humiliated beyond endurance,
will not be appeased, they want
nothing! abhor the common food,
push it away imperiously, command

a better thing, then fetch it themselves
from the box; their frustrated wills conjoin
with a guilt—that is a frenzy! Now
unbearable to think two thoughts at once.

4

Who is the child who will not eat?
Who knows her name? Can't she be found?
She is a secret, breakfast and dinner
preferring death; turning away,
saying nothing, unhappy child.

5

The little girls are calling the big girls
about them, for instruction, to play house
and teach them to behave—out in the backyard.
Why do you linger in a corner and won't play,
your black hair curling, eyes sullen, trembling,
thin? Ghost already? Your breath so bitter?
They want you for mother, calling in flat voices
stiff with light, Play with us! Play with *us!*
So shy of the light, you stoop to tie something
with a sudden erratic energy, hiding
your face, your fingers tighten, you drift away.
Excited, the children rush forward
shouting, Here's the baby bird again!

6

Hungry for destinies, if only
to find a crust, I follow.
Starving, if I demand of you,

will I be fed?
Past the broken ring of children
jumping in place, calling; concealed,
you lean your head on the tree,
stepmother to yourself, waif, and groom.
Gathered to bless the emptiness,
you impersonate a family,
giving, taking, in the perpetual
moment, impossible wine.
Faltering, jarred, reaching,
what do you see? Quick,
your secret, is it a destiny?
Is something fulfilled?
Louder! What are you saying?
That you're urgently, mortally *hungry*?

7

A sparrow hops to the plate.
The past is a crumb to him.
He flies away. He comes back.
He eats it, miraculous food!
Children totter at him, exploding their hands.
He flies off. A circle is completed.
They put out a second morsel.
Eternity is this crumb to him.
He possesses and divides it,
fulfilling the law.
Accursed, all parents cry
that all they have done is useless,
the unjustifiable bread unblessed!
You have cast a profaneness everywhere
but on these children, sacred for your sake.

Almost at dawn, she babbles
the names of her childhood,
precious dolls dressed up
because they have to please:
Let go! Don't touch! Stop it!
Well, they guard her too,
though spiteful at times and nasty
and wanting always to have
their toes kissed. Tumbled hair
has touched her sleep. It is such
a little way to go . . . if the dolls
do not mislead. A breeze
feathers her hair. Hush it! Oh why
is the soul sent on errands
in the dark? with its list
of names, its fist of pennies,
its beating heart? Why, to buy
an egg, of course. See,
hen hides her egg under
the sycamore tree—smart girl!
The meadownight smiles and
rolls over in sleep. Startled,
in flight, all ears, she stares
from its edge at the old ladies
under parasols dragging
the morass of their legs.
Their smiles are tranquil and tiny,
solicit her to come
over to them. Heartbroken,
she bolts from the death-wall,
outspeeds her reckless body

that runs on its flittering shadow.
Arrow, what do you desire?
Nothing Everything Nothing
—I was born on the empty air,
cloud tops were my cradle,
and I am two, and one, and two.
To have been a child is such
responsibility—to keep
those old people from dying
you may have to stay child forever.
Who-am-I? is pretending she's
asleep, the lazy thing!
Who-was-I? makes herself
useful and carries the names
for her in a special box.
And whom will the child marry?
for marry she must. If ever
I marry, it will be
no one named in any book
ever written or read. *Who-will-
I-be?* is someone else's
doll, displeases her, she will
say a bad word to it,
and throw it down, and refuse
to look back.

To waken you, Carmen
Fidela, with your name,
I linger at your sleep's side, but
can I be gentle enough
touching you with these beams?

the day asks. And it *is*
day, called so by every chance.
Then happily the arrow climbs
to the height and sees that all
is there abiding faithfully
in the light with open eyes.
Awake, my dawn, my daughter,
sings the day, I have no
tenderness that is not you,
no distance untouched by you
idling and singing here,
for whose sake I have
abandoned the night.
I am no longer dreaming,
she says, but have I done
what I set out to do?
Both now and never,
it is you, says the day,
you and none other
entirely in this light.
Day, touch me, call me again!
she cries a second time,
for I wish to awake.